This book belongs to _____

_____

DRAWING AND COLOURING WITH ELVIS ANIMAL ALPHABET

Eric Reeves

MAPLE
PUBLISHERS

First Published in 2021

ISBN: 978-1-914366-03-1

Copyright © Maple Publishers

Cover by: White Magic Studios

Illustrated by: White Magic Studios

Designed by: White Magic Studios

Published by: Maple Publishers
1 Brunel Way, Slough, SL1 1FQ
www.maplepublishers.com

Scan the QR Code
to visit
Roving Genius at YouTube

A CIP catalogue record for this title is available from the British Library.

All rights reserved. No part of this book may be reproduced or translated by any form or by any means, electronic or mechanical, including photocopying, recording or by any information storage and retrieval system without written permission from the author.

Let us have fun colouring with Elvis.

Colour the ape. Use the right colours.

Apes and monkeys look alike, but they are different. Monkeys have tails, apes do not have tails.

Let us have fun colouring with Elvis.

Colour the bird. Use the right colours.

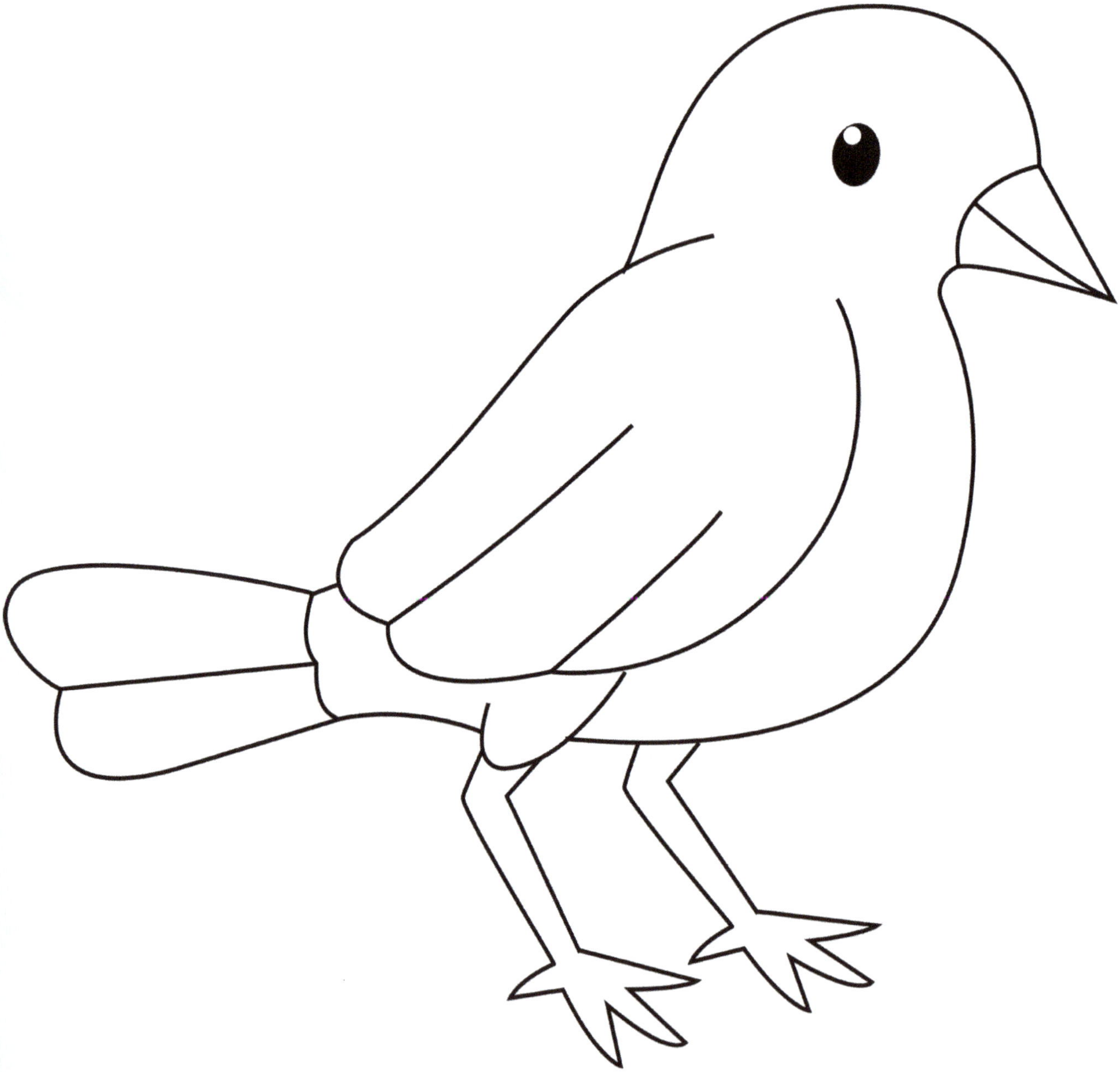

Birds have hollow bones that help them fly.

Let us have fun colouring with Elvis.

Colour the caterpillar. Use the right colours.

Caterpillars grow up and turn into butterflies.

Let us have fun colouring with Elvis.

Colour the dolphin. Use the right colours.

Dolphins are sharp and intelligent, and are very friendly animals.

Let us have fun colouring with Elvis.

Colour the emu. Use the right colours.

Emus are the second largest bird in the world after ostrich, and have two sets of eyelids.

Let us have fun colouring with Elvis.

Colour the flamingo. Use the right colours.

Flamingos have pink legs which can be longer than their entire body.

Drawing and Colouring with Elvis – Animal Alphabet

©MAPLE PUBLISHERS

Let us have fun colouring with Elvis.

Colour the goat. Use the right colours.

Goats are expert in climbing and can climb to the top of trees.

Let us have fun colouring with Elvis.

Colour the hippo. Use the right colours.

H

Hippos love to be in water or mud to remain cool; they are most active at night and eat grass.

Let us have fun colouring with Elvis.

Colour the iguana. Use the right colours.

Iguanas' use their tail as whips to drive off enemies.

Let us have fun colouring with Elvis.

Colour the jelly fish. Use the right colours.

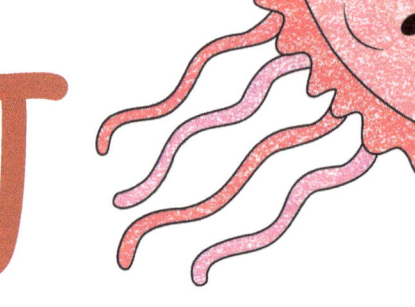

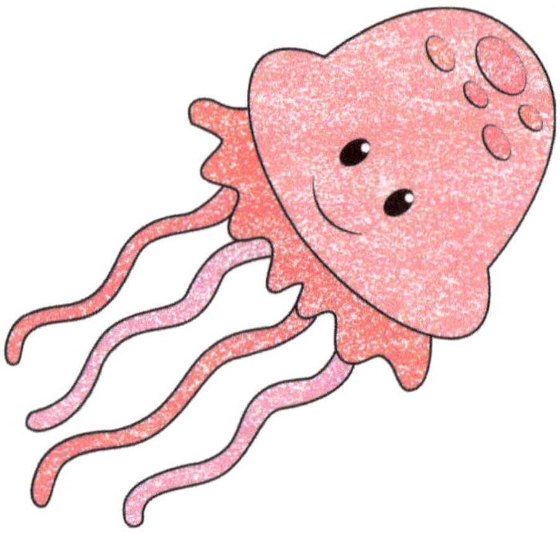

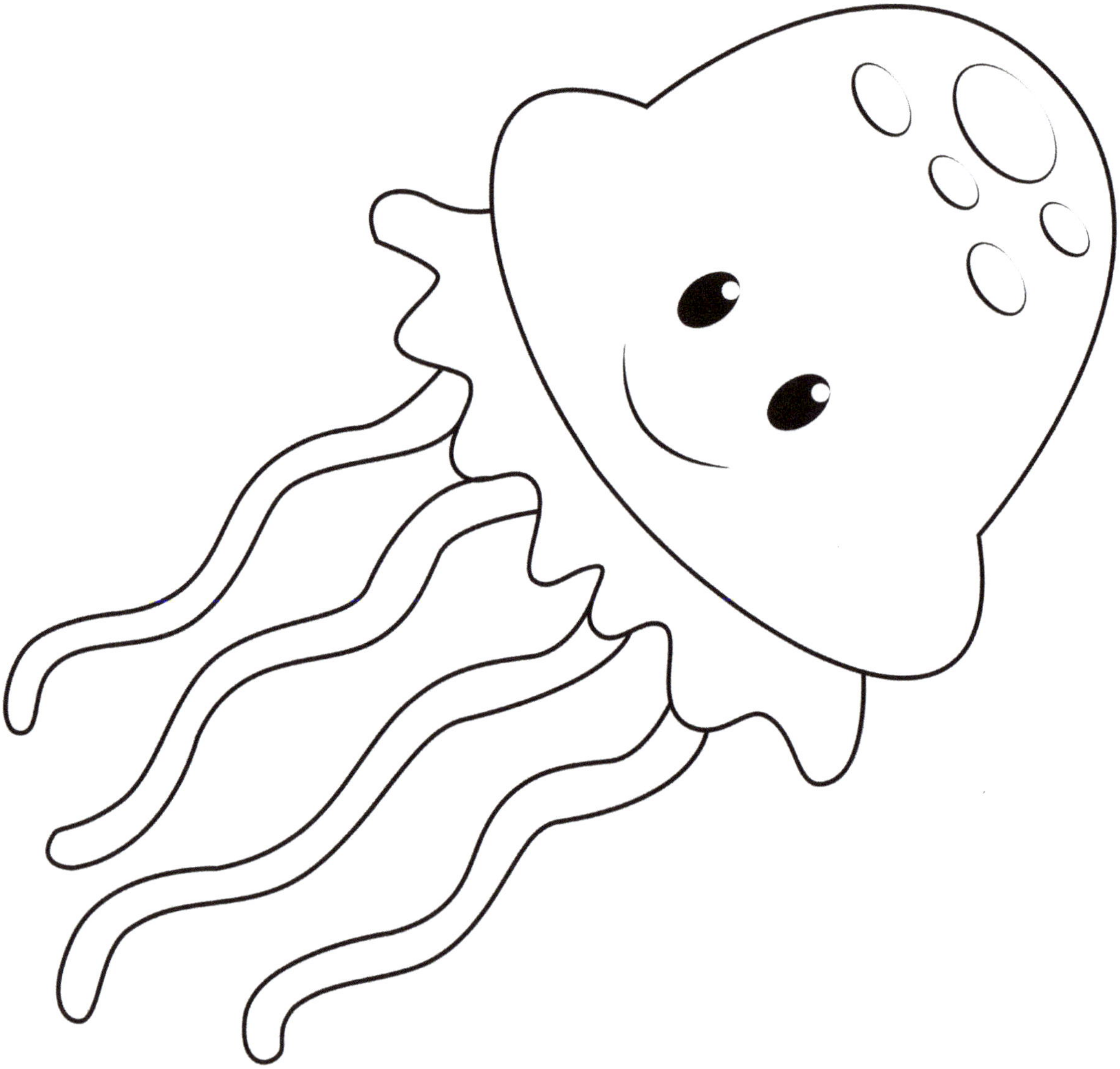

Jellyfish aren't actually fish, and their stings are very painful and sometimes dangerous for humans.

Let us have fun colouring with Elvis.

Colour the kingfisher. Use the right colours.

Kingfishers are brightly coloured birds, and hunt for fish by swooping down and plunging into the water.

Let us have fun colouring with Elvis.

Colour the lion. Use the right colours.

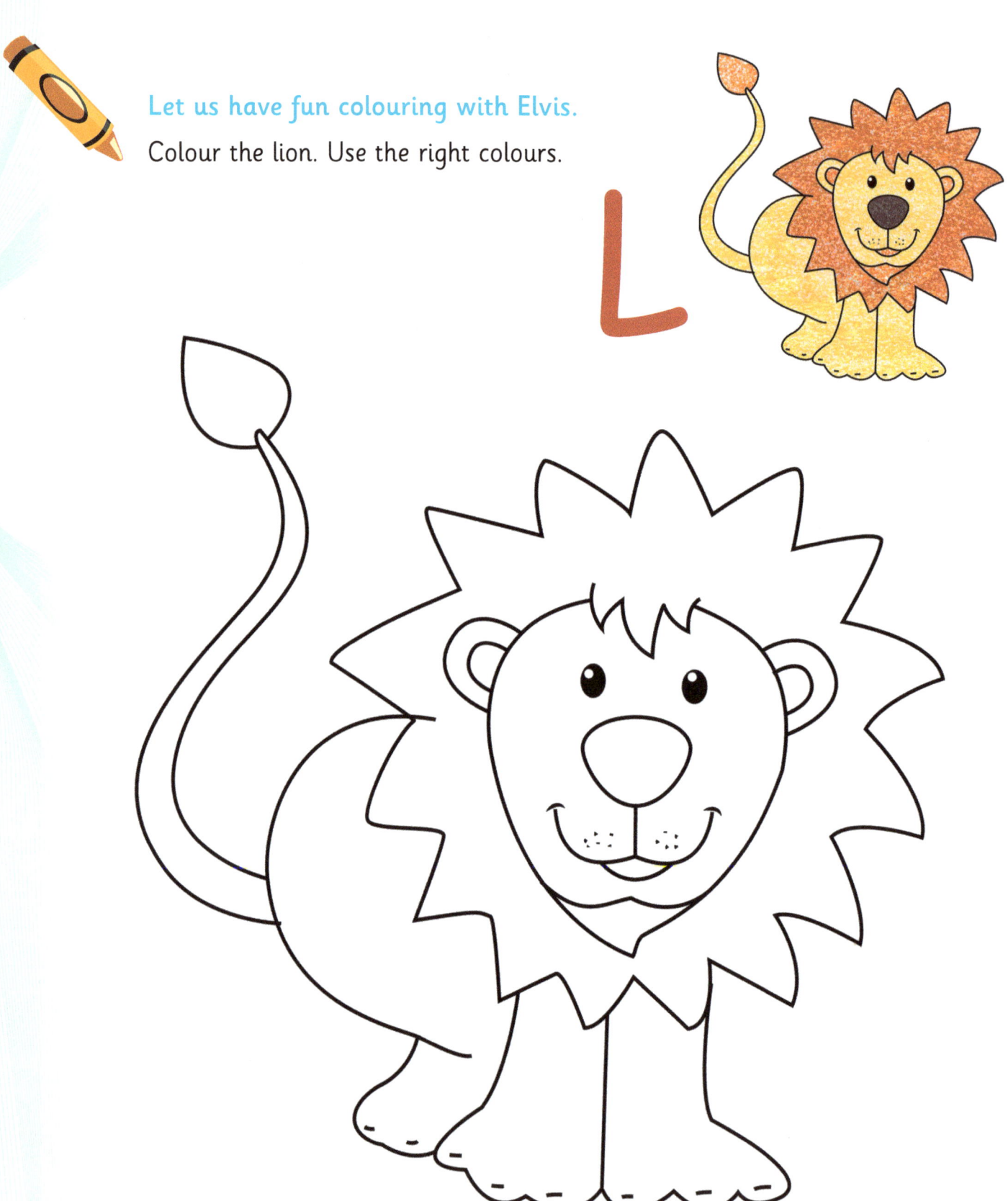

Lion roars and is known as the king of the jungle but sleeps for 16-20 hours.

Let us have fun colouring with Elvis.

Colour the magpie. Use the right colours.

Magpies are clever and intelligent birds with long tails. A group of magpies is sometimes described as "a parliament."

Let us have fun colouring with Elvis.

Colour the nightingale. Use the right colours.

N

Nightingales are small birds known for their powerful and beautiful songs. They live in the woodlands and prefer low bushes to tall trees.

Let us have fun colouring with Elvis.

Colour the octopus. Use the right colours.

Octopuses pile up anything they can find rocks, shells, broken glass and even bottle caps. They live alone in dens made of rocks by themselves.

Let us have fun colouring with Elvis.

Colour the penguin. Use the right colours.

P

Penguins are aquatic flightless birds and spend around half their time in water and the other half on land.

Let us have fun colouring with Elvis.

Colour the quail. Use the right colours.

Quails are small, plump birds and its fun to see mother quails walking through the grasslands and their babies trailing behind them.

Let us have fun colouring with Elvis.

Colour the reindeer. Use the right colours.

Reindeer can't fly, they can run, but they do sometimes have red noses.

Let us have fun colouring with Elvis.

Colour the squirrel. Use the right colours.

Squirrels are commonly seen everywhere and are terrific climbers; they can make great leaps between branches.

Let us have fun colouring with Elvis.

Colour the turtle. Use the right colours.

T

Turtles lay eggs and can hide their heads inside the shells when attacked by predators.

Let us have fun colouring with Elvis.

Colour the unicorn. Use the right colours.

U

Unicorns are believed to be legendary and pure creatures with magical powers.

Let us have fun colouring with Elvis.

Colour the vulture. Use the right colours.

Vultures feed on the remains of dead animals and do not hunt for food.

Let us have fun colouring with Elvis.

Colour the woodpecker. Use the right colours.

W

Woodpeckers have tough pointed beaks and use them to hammer into trees for insects and for chiselling nest.

Let us have fun colouring with Elvis.

Colour the x-ray fish. Use the right colours.

X-ray fish is a small fish with transparent skin and we can see its organ and skeleton, just like an X-ray.

Let us have fun colouring with Elvis.

Colour the yak. Use the right colours.

Yaks are friendly to people they know and can swim in almost frozen waters, and when necessary they can even obtain water by eating snow.

Let us have fun colouring with Elvis.

Colour the zebra. Use the right colours.

Z

Zebra crossings or pedestrian crossings are named after the black and white stripes of zebras.